POETRY AND CRITICISM

Poetry and Criticism

By

Edith Sitwell 1887.

New York

Henry Holt and Company

POETRY AND CRITICISM

POETRY AND CRITICISM

ABRAHAM COWLEY, in his Preface to *Poems*, 1656, says: "If wit be such a plant that it scarce receives heat enough to preserve it alive even in the summer of our cold climate, how can it choose but wither in a long and a sharp winter? A warlike, various, and a tragical age is best to *write of*, but worst to *write in*." Whether this age, the most warlike, various, and tragical that our country has ever known, will flower into the virtues of future poets, I know not; but this I do know—that it has produced a sparse few great poets, and that it is a time of budding, like an early and cold spring. And, too, it is a time of turmoil and strife in the minds of poets—one of those ages which recurs, once every hundred years or so, when the poets must examine the claims of tradition, as far as the technique of poetry is concerned. For in every age of civilised times, or at any rate since the time of Shakespeare, we find poets discussing these problems of poetry and defending innovations in various Prefaces and Defences of Poetry. For instance, we know that Thomas Lodge published a *Defence of Poetry* in 1579, and Sir Philip Sidney an *Apology for Poetry* about the year 1583; Ben Jonson treated of the problems of poetry in his *Discoveries*, and Thomas Campion wrote his *Observations on the Art of English Poesy* in 1602. A little later, Sir William Davenant's theories, in his Preface to *Gondibert*, roused an answer from Thomas Hobbes. In this essay, Hobbes, irritated by the nonsense that is sometimes talked about inspiration, gibes at "the foolish custom by which a man, enabled to speak wisely from the principles of nature and his own meditation, loves rather to be thought to speak by inspiration, like a bagpipe."

It is still more amusing, for poets on whom Mr. J. C. Squire tries to impose his "dry" régime, to read Samuel Daniel's *Defence of Rhyme*, written in contradiction of Campion's theories, for it contains passages which really might have been written by Mr. Squire himself—sentences such as this: "Suffer . . . the world to enjoy that which it likes, and what it knows, seeing that whatsoever force of words doth move, delight, and sway the affections of men, in what Scythian sort soever it be disposed or uttered, that is true number, measure, eloquence, and the perfection of speech;

4

which I said had as many shapes as there be tongues
or nations in the world, nor can with all the tyran-
nical rules of idle rhetoric be governed otherwise
than custom and present observation will allow.'
It is easy to deduce from this that criticism has not
changed—excepting in becoming more vulgar.
For at least, in the centuries of which we speak,
poetry was regarded as an art, and not as a vehicle
for conveying misty moral ideas; it was not con-
founded with inferior metaphysics in the minds of
the people, nor was it allowed that poetry should
be the flimsy, unshaped outpourings of an emotion
which would shame men in real life, or if it were
represented upon a canvas. In those halcyon
days criticism was regarded as the prerogative of
the poet and the man of letters; it was for them
to prove what poetry should be and how it should
be written, and even when these men of letters
shrank from progress, at least they had some lucid
and informed (even though misguided) reason for
doing so. It was not until the times of Pope and
Dryden that the real trouble began; but even
then matters were not so intolerable as they are
at present, when the illiterate writers of musical
comedies, revues, and salacious plays, and, with
them, the writers of the Yellow Press, believe
themselves to be competent to act as critics of

literature. In a paper of the Yellow Press, a short while ago, an article appeared claiming that the English people have always been notable for "seeing through" and exposing charlatans and impostors in literature and the arts. This is very true, since they have, in their time, seen through and rendered life intolerable to such charlatans and impostors as Coleridge, Keats, Shelley, and Wordsworth, and, before he was frightened into conforming to their ideals, Tennyson.

Let us examine how these great poets of the past were treated. De Quincey, in the first edition of *The Confessions of an English Opium-Eater*, quotes a passage from Wordsworth, but does not name the author, saying merely that they are lines from "a great modern poet." Then, in a later edition of the *Confessions*, De Quincey adds this note: "From a great modern poet. . . . What poet? It was Wordsworth; and why did I not formally name him? This throws a light backwards upon the strange history of Wordsworth's reputation. The year in which I wrote and published these *Confessions* was 1821; and at that time the name of Wordsworth, though beginning to emerge from the dark cloud of scorn and contumely which had hitherto overshadowed it, was yet most imperfectly established. Not

6

until ten years later was his greatness cheerfully and generally acknowledged. I therefore, as the very earliest (without one exception) of all who came forward, in the beginning of his career, to honour and welcome him, shrank with disgust from making any sentence of mine the occasion for an explosion of vulgar malice against him. But the grandeur of the passage here cited inevitably spoke for itself, and he that would have been most scornful on hearing the name of the poet coupled with the epithet of 'great,' could not but find his malice intercepted and himself cheated into cordial admiration by the splendour of the verses."

From this passage we understand that Wordsworth, who was born in 1770, was abominated and insulted until 1821, when he was fifty-one years of age, and barely tolerated for another ten years, until he was sixty-one. He was then, I presume, allowed to live in peace for the remaining nineteen years of his life. Let us transfer ourselves in imagination to 1821, the year when *The Confessions of an English Opium-Eater* saw the light. Mr. Harold Monro reminds us, in the *Chapbook* of 1923, that "*Hyperion* was published in 1820, *Prometheus Unbound* in 1821. The genius of Wordsworth was in hot dispute.

"In 1817, however, Moore had been paid three thousand guineas for *Lalla Rookh*. Critical literature had recently been enriched by such works as *Biographia Literaria*, and Wordsworth's unparalleled essays and prefaces. . . . But the Mr. Squire . . . and Mr. Lynd of that moment found mediocrity no less comfortably attractive, and while they were ardently agreeing to differ or agreeing to agree about Moore, Campbell, Kirke White, Bloomfield, Hogg, Southey, and others, many of the works that were destined later to represent the genius of the time unconsciously eluded them or were consciously dismissed."

It is, indeed, interesting to examine Campbell's enormous anthology of poetry. Campbell was, at least, a contemporary of Wordsworth and Coleridge, though he was fifteen years older than Shelley. Yet in this anthology the bulk of the poems are the dead, neat, flat, comfortable, safe works of William Shenstone and poets of the like kind. The abuse to which the great poets of this time were subjected was only equalled by the neglect. Here are some of the criticisms they were obliged to bear.

"*The Rime of the Ancient Mariner*," said the *Monthly Review*, "seems a rhapsody of unintelligible wildness and incoherence, of which we do not perceive the drift, unless the joke lies in depriving the guest of his share of the feast."

"At first," said the *Quarterly*, "it appeared to us that Mr. Keats had been amusing himself and wearying his readers with an immeasurable game of *bouts-rimés*; but, if we recollect right, it is an indispensable condition of this play that the rhymes, when filled up, shall have a meaning; and our author, as we have already hinted, has no meaning."

Now take Jeffrey, of the *Edinburgh Review*. "The volume before us (Wordsworth's *The Excursion*), if we were to describe it very shortly, we should characterise it as a tissue of moral and devotional ravings, in which innumerable changes are hung upon a few very simple and familiar ideas; but with such an accompaniment of long words, long sentences, and unwieldy phrases— such a hubbub of strained raptures and fantastical sublimities—that it is often extremely difficult for the most skilful and attentive student to obtain a glimpse of the author's meaning, and altogether impossible for an ordinary reader to conjecture what he is about."

Blackwood says of Shelley's *Prometheus Unbound*: "To our apprehension it is little else but absolute raving; and, were we not assured to the contrary, we should take it for granted that the author is lunatic, as his principles are ludicrously wicked, and his poetry a *mélange* of nonsense, cockneyism, poverty, and pedantry."

The *Monthly Magazine* says of Keats' poems: "The faults characteristic of his school are still held up with as much affectation by Mr. Keats as if he were fearful of not coming in for his due share of singularity, obscurity, and conceit."

But one of the hardest thrashings poets received at this time was from Thomas Peacock in his *The Four Ages of Poetry*. Here is a passage from this amusing, though disgracefully misguided, essay: "Thomson and Cowper looked at the trees and hills which so many ingenious gentlemen had rhymed about so long without looking at them at all, and the effect of the operation upon poetry was like the discovery of a new world. Painting showed the influence, and the principles of picturesque beauty were explored by adventurous essayists with indefatigable pertinacity. The success which attended these experiments, and the pleasure which resulted from them, had the usual effect of all new enthusiasms—that of turning the heads of a few unfortunate persons, the patriarchs of the age of brass, who, mistaking the prominent novelty for the all-important totality, seem to have ratiocinated much in the following manner: 'Poetical genius is the finest of all things, and we feel we have more of it than anybody ever had. The way to bring it to perfection is to cultivate poetical impressions exclusively. Poetical impressions can be received only among natural scenes; for all that is artificial is anti-poetical. Society is artificial, therefore we will live out of society. The mountains are natural, therefore we will live in the mountains. There we shall be shining models of purity and virtue, passing the whole day in the innocent and amiable occupations of going up and down hill, receiving poetical impressions, and communicating them in immortal verse to admiring generations.' To some such perversion of intellect we owe that egregious confraternity of rhymesters, known by the name of the Lake Poets, who certainly did receive and communicate to the world some of the most extraordinary poetical impressions that were ever heard of, and ripened into models of public virtue too splendid to need illustration. . . . This gave a new tone to poetry and conjured up a herd of desperate imitators, who have brought the age of brass prematurely to its dotage."

Forty-four years later we find Alfred Lord Tennyson, or, as he was at that time, Alfred Tennyson, Esq., P.L., D.C.L., in trouble. And what was he in trouble about? He was in trouble about the disgraceful character of his poem *Enoch Arden*. We find the *Englishwoman's Magazine* of 1864 standing up for him with the utmost courage as follows:

"Some of our contemporaries have worked themselves up into a very silly passion about Tennyson telling a story which turns upon 'bigamy' as the foundation of a work of art. But this is simply calling names. . . . Now what is the essence of the thing called bigamy? We beg pardon for reproducing such a coarse word, but no choice is left to us by the critics who have chosen to attack Mr. Tennyson upon the 'morality' of his poem. What, we ask, is the essence of the crime in question? . . . And what will readers who have been accustomed to trust reviews, especially respectable ones, what *will* they say when we inform them that Annie Lee does nothing of the kind? The poem states in the most explicit manner that the wife has been *twelve years* without hearing of her husband. This alone absolves her, according to the well-known unrepealed statute of George IV. But what is more, the poor woman must be held to be morally, as well as legally, absolved, for she takes pains to obtain guidance from Heaven, if possible—superstitious pains, but the best that occurred to her. She had recourse to what is known as sortilege; her Bible opened twice at a particular text. . . ."

All this is most interesting, both as throwing a light upon the critics and as throwing a light upon Lord Tennyson.

There is not the slightest difference between the criticisms of the past and the criticisms of to-day, excepting that the latter are more vulgar, and often more personally abusive. I do not, naturally, refer to those critics, men and women of profound and delicate insight, intelligence, and knowledge, to whom I, and all other poets, owe so much, but rather to those persons who, with no knowledge of poetry, wish to insult personally the poets whose work they cannot understand. But the critics are not always unkind.

Here is a criticism from the *Sunday Times* of 17th May 1925, showing exactly the same friendliness towards tame, safe verse that has always prevailed in England.

"The poet's (Mr. Edward Shanks') work has lost none of its sweetness and artistry; it is, as always, quietly ascetic and lucid. Mr. Shanks *never startles*." (The italics are mine.) "He plays a game that children play, tracing a shadow on the wall:

'Until at last the lamp is brought,
The game is done, and now I see
The tangled scribble I have wrought
Grimacing at me mockingly.'

But the revelation is, after all, *an unexpected one, and not such as to disturb the most mobile placidity.* A peculiar quality of certain types of the English countryside is made manifest in Mr. Shanks' descriptive verse:

'But never a footstep comes to trouble
The rooks among the new-sown corn,
Or pigeons rising from the stubble,
And flashing brighter as they roam.'"

In savage criticisms (as also in this), the true function of the critic is set aside. Ben Jonson in his *Discoveries* says: "The office of a true critic or censor is not to throw by a letter anywhere, or damn an innocent syllable, but lay the words together and amend them; judge sincerely of the author and his matter, which is the sign of solid and perfect learning in a man. Such was Horace, an author of much civility . . . an excellent and true judge upon cause and reason, not because he thought so, but because he knew so out of use and experience."

I think it cannot be denied that one of the principal reasons why certain critics, and a large part of the public, feel unable to understand the aims of modernist poets, is that these poets are leaving the tradition that leads from Wordsworth, and are returning to an earlier line in poetry. With the advent of Wordsworth the tradition of English poetry was changed, and it is understandable, therefore, that those people who, while they never read poetry, are so well fitted to judge of it, cannot see the tradition in modernist poetry, since they are only conversant with the line of poetry we have inherited from Wordsworth, and with that other tradition formed by the pre-Raphaelite poets, though this could scarcely be called a new line, since, before it, we had Keats. Many of the poets labelled Georgian are still writing in the manner and from the same point of view as that which has prevailed since Wordsworth, and therefore seem less obscure and alarming to a certain portion of the press and of the public.

Every hundred years or so it becomes necessary for a change to take place in the body of poetry, otherwise the health and the force that should invigorate it fade. Then a fresh movement appears and produces a few great men, and once more the force and the vigour die from the results of age; the movement is carried on by weak and worthless imitators, and a change becomes necessary again. Because fresh life and vigour, and therefore change, become necessary to poetry, it does not mean that the old poets are less reverenced by the new. This change enriches the blood; it does not destroy the old, but it creates the new. With Wordsworth a fresh channel was brought into English poetry, for he insisted upon the right of a poet to bring the language of ordinary speech, the actions of common life, into poetry. In the Preface to *Lyrical Ballads* (1800-5) we find him urging this claim with passion and beauty: "Poetry sheds no tears 'such as angels weep,' but natural and human tears; she can boast of no celestial ichor that distinguishes her vital juices from those of prose; the same human blood circulates through them both." Then in a note he writes: "I here use the word 'Poetry' (though against my own judgment) as opposed to the word Prose, and synonymous with metrical composition. But much confusion has been introduced by this contradistinction of poetry and

16

prose, instead of the more philosophical one of poetry and matter of fact or science. The only strict antithesis to prose is metre. Nor is this, in truth, a *strict* antithesis, because lines and passages of metre so naturally occur in writing prose that it would be scarcely possible to avoid them, even if it were desirable."

Wordsworth battled for these principles and the cause of liberty during the whole of his life; but, unfortunately, that liberty has by now been carried too far in some cases, and his argument that poetry is not an antithesis to prose has now been used as an excuse for the most monstrous excesses of dullness. It is therefore time that we returned to an earlier tradition in poetry, and left the peasant and words suitable to the peasant. Let us for a moment examine the new poetry to which so many people take exception, and we shall find in much of it the great tradition leading from the Elizabethans. This couplet is not from an early seventeenth-century poem, yet it might well have been:

> "Leave the spangled waters and lie down to sleep
> Beneath these boughs that never cease to weep."

I will not say the name of the poet who wrote those lines, for the same reason that prevented

De Quincey from divulging the name of the poet whose verses he quoted.

Again, free verse is by many people supposed to be a vehicle for conveying the sense, sound, and delight of slaughter-houses and factories, and it is supposed also to be a formless affair. But let us take other lines from the poem quoted above—these lines, for instance:

"Such are the clouds.
  They float with white coolness and snowy shade,
  Sometimes preening their flightless feathers.
  Float, proud swans, on the calm lake
  And wave your clipped wings in the azure air,
  Then arch your neck and look into the deep for pearls.
  Now can you drink dew from tall trees and sloping
    fields of heaven,
  Gather new coolness for to-morrow's heat,
  And sleep through the soft night with folded wing."

It is extraordinary that anyone reading this should not realise the quality of the poetry. This is partly due, of course, to the fact that there is a general lack of interest in the fabric of poetry. Many people have no feeling for or knowledge of that quality which my friend Mr. Robert Graves calls "texture." "The term texture," says Mr. Graves in his invaluable *Contemporary Techniques of Poetry*, "covers the relations of a poem's vowels and consonants, other than rhymes, considered as mere sound, and supplementing the rhythm and images. It will . . . include the variation of internal vowel-sounds to give an effect of richness; the use, perhaps, of liquid consonants and labials and open vowels to give smoothness, of aspirate and dentals to give force, of gutturals to give strength; the careful use of sibilants, which are to texture what salt is to food." It is because of this insensitiveness to texture that most people do not realise that Alexander Pope's *The Rape of the Lock* is one of the most beautiful, as it is one of the most skilful, poems in the English language. The texture of this poem is so airy that it might have been spun by one of the Sylphs of whom it speaks. But this airy quality is as much a matter of texture as of inspiration, as much a question of inspiration as of texture. Indeed, if the time ever comes when this poem is valued at its true worth, I shall feel more hopeful for the future of English poetry. And for this reason *The Rape of the Lock* is one of the most beautiful examples of the fusion of subject-matter and style, without which perfection in a poem is impossible. De Quincey, in his essay on "Style," tells us of a conversation with Wordsworth, in which he said that "it is the highest degree unphilosophic to call language or diction 'the dress of thoughts.' " He would call it "the incarnation of thoughts." And De Quincey goes on to say: "Never in one word was so profound a truth conveyed . . . and the truth is apparent on consideration; for, if language were merely a dress, then you could separate the two; you could lay the thoughts on the left hand, the language on the right. But, generally speaking, you can no more deal thus with poetic thoughts than you can with soul and body. The union is too subtle, the inter-texture too ineffable, each co-existing not merely *with* the other, but each *in* and *through* the other. An image, for instance, a single word, often enters into a thought as a constituent part. In short, the two elements are not united as a body with a separable dress, but as a mysterious incarnation."

The time having come when a change once more becomes necessary to the vision and fabric of poetry, certain people follow the example of their forebears and do everything in their power to hinder the progress of the poets. Yet when the modern poet is blamed for innovations in technique, in vision, and in manner, let us remember that such men as Ben Jonson, Milton, Coleridge, Wordsworth, and Shelley defended innovations in technique and originality of vision with the utmost passion. Ben Jonson, in his *Discoveries*, says: "To all the observations of the ancients we have our own experience. It is true, they opened the gates and made the way that went before us; but as guides, not as commanders. Truth lies open to all; it is no man's several." Again, in the same work, we find: "I am not of that opinion to conclude a poet's liberty within the narrow limit of laws which either the grammarians or the philosophers prescribe. For, before they found out those laws, there were many excellent poets that fulfilled them; amongst whom none more perfect than Sophocles, who lived a little before Aristotle." On the same subject, Milton, in his *Reason of Church Government*, argues "whether the laws of Aristotle herein are strictly to be kept, or Nature to be followed, which, in them that know art and use judgment, is no transgression, but an enriching of art." Dryden says: "Better a mechanic rule were stretched or broken than a great beauty were omitted." Shelley, in his *Defence of Poetry*, says: "An observation of the regular mode of the recurrence of harmony in the language of poetical minds, together with its relation to music, produce metre, or a certain system of traditional forms of harmony and language. Yet it is by no means essential that a poet should accommodate his language to this traditional form, so that the harmony, which is its spirit, be observed. The practice is indeed convenient and popular and to be preferred, especially in such composition as includes much action; but every great poet must inevitably innovate upon the example of his predecessors in the exact structure of his peculiar versification."

There is, undoubtedly, a vast difficulty for fresh readers in the fact that modernist poetry is bringing a new and heightened consciousness to life; and this fresh perception of natural objects comes, sometimes, as a shock to people who are used to taking their impressions at second-hand—to people who want comfort and not the truth. The senses of many people are practically unused—not through their fault, but because they have been taught that inherited ideas are the best. The result of this is that there is no connection between their senses and their brain, and it irritates them excessively when these are brought into relation with each other. The modernist poet's brain is becoming a central sense, interpreting and controlling the other five senses; for he has learned the truth uttered by Blake, that "Man has no body distinct from his soul, for that called body is a portion of soul discerned by the five senses, the chief inlets of soul in this age." His senses have become broadened and cosmopolitanised; they are no longer little islands, speaking only their own narrow language, living their sleepy life alone. When the speech of one sense is insufficient to convey his entire meaning, he uses the language of another. He knows, too, that every sight, touch, sound, smell of the world we live in has its meaning; and it is the poet's duty to interpret those meanings.

Modernist poets are not difficult to follow if the fact of different sense-values is remembered. Let us, as an example of this new scale of sense-values, use an "Aubade" by a modern poet—a poem which many people pretended was incapable of an explanation. Whereas it is, in reality, extremely simple and quite explainable.

AUBADE

"Jane, Jane,
    Tall as a crane,
    The morning light creaks down again.

Comb your cockscomb-ragged hair,
Jane, Jane, come down the stair.

Each dull, blunt wooden stalactite
Of rain creaks, hardened by the light,

23

Sounding like an overtone
From some lonely world unknown.

But the creaking, empty light
Will never harden into sight,

Will never penetrate your brain
With overtones like the blunt rain.

The light would show, if it could harden,
Eternities of kitchen garden,

Cockscomb flowers that none will pluck,
And wooden flowers that 'gin to cluck.

In the kitchen you must light
Flames as staring red and white

As carrots or as turnips—shining
Where the cold dawn light lies whining.

Cockscomb hair on the cold wind
Hangs limp, turns the milk's weak mind.

Jane, Jane,
Tall as a crane,
The morning light creaks down again."

"The morning light creaks down again." The
author said "creaks" because, in a very early
dawn, after rain, the light has a curious uncer-
tain quality, as though it does not run quite
smoothly. Also, it falls in hard cubes, squares,
and triangles, which, again, give one the impres-

sion of a creaking sound, because of the association with wood. *"Each dull, blunt wooden stalactite of rain creaks, hardened by the light."* In the early dawn, long raindrops are transformed by the light, until they have the light's own quality of hardness; also they have the dull and blunt and tasteless quality of wood; as they move in the wind, they seem to creak. *"Sounding like an overtone from some lonely world unknown."* Though it seems to us as though we heard them sensorily, yet the sound is unheard in reality; it has the quality of an overtone from some unknown and mysterious world. *"But the creaking, empty light will never harden into sight, will never penetrate your brain with overtones like the blunt rain."* The poem is about a country servant, a girl on a farm, plain and neglected and unhappy, and with a sad bucolic stupidity, coming down in the dawn to light the fire; and this phrase means that to her poor mind the light is an empty thing which conveys nothing. It cannot bring sight to her—she is not capable of seeing anything; it can never bring overtones to her mind, because she is not capable of hearing them. She scarcely knows even that she is suffering. *"The light would show, if it could harden, eternities of kitchen garden, cockscomb flowers that none will pluck, and wooden flowers that 'gin to cluck."* If she were capable of seeing anything, still she would only see the whole of eternity as the world of kitchen gardens to which she is accustomed, with flowers red and lank as cockscombs (uncared for, just as she is uncared for), and those hard flowers that dip and bend beneath the rain till they look (and seem as though they must sound) like hens clucking. *"In the kitchen you must light flames as staring red and white as carrots or as turnips—shining where the cold dawn light lies whining."* To the author's sight, the shivering movement of a certain cold dawn light upon the floor suggests a kind of high animal whining or whimpering, a kind of half-frightened and subservient urge to something outside our consciousness. *"Cockscomb hair on the cold wind hangs limp, turns the milk's weak mind,"* is obviously a joke, and a joke may be permitted even to a poet.

Critics complain of the themes that modern poets choose, themes which appear occasionally as flippant. On this subject Jean Cocteau writes: "The music-hall, the circus, and American ragtime bands, all these things fertilise an artist just as life does. To turn to one's account the emotions aroused by this sort of entertainment is not to derive art from art. These entertainments are not art; they stimulate in the same way as machinery, animals, natural scenery, or danger." Indeed, where is the poet to go? What comfort can he take? He is obliged, if he speaks truth, to show the world in all its triviality. He can speak of nobility also, but he would not be doing his duty if he spoke only of nobility. He must show how, through fear of life, many souls are becoming part of the stocks and stones. Therefore he writes of flower-shows where, in the coral tents of the noonday light, we can barter for the no longer disastrous stars, potted out in earthenware. The people, glazed by the heat, dance to little tunes that are bright and yellow and blatant as calceolarias. No time for darkness there, excepting in the cubes of their musical-box brains, as they dance in the ephemeral sunshine. The poet writes of those flower-shows in the countrysides where Destiny is befouled, and has feathers like a hen, in landscapes where the leaves have an animal fleshiness, and old pig-snouted Darkness grunts and roots in the hovels. There the country gentlemen's lives are rooted in the mould, and they know that beyond the sensual aspects of the sky (that harsh and goatish tent) something hides, but they have forgotten what it is. So they wander,

27

aiming with their guns at mocking feathered crea-
tures that have learnt the wonder and secret of
movement, beneath clouds that are so low hung
that they seem nothing but wooden potting-sheds
for the no longer disastrous stars that win the
prize at the local flower-show. The water of the
shallow lake gurgles like a stoat, murderously; the
little unfledged feathers of the foam have forgotten how to fly; and the country gentlemen wander, hunting for something, hunting.

Then, again, the poet writes of the kind of no-
bodies we find in the memoirs of the present, no-
bodies more gilded and more numerous than the
sands of the shore. They roll together, and their
little dry whispers overcome and deaden the sound
of all the leaves in Pan's forests. So the poets
write of this new aristocracy that is an aristocracy
neither of brains nor of tradition—a race of dwarfs
on stilts, inhabiting hotels carved to look like
clouds, clouds carved to look like hotels. And the
poets write of the little children by the swan-
bosomed shore of the sea, watching the side-
shows to be seen upon the sand—a Punch and
Judy show, bright coloured as the winter sun, or
a marionette show. We were children like that
once, long ago, made unhappy and terrified by the
unconscious cruelty of those puppets' fate, pulled

backwards and forwards as they were, to love, to hate, to murder, to annihilation, by the mechanical actions of that ragged Hunger, the showman.

Modern poets are building among the common movements of life, just as Wordsworth built, only the modern poet has a different stylisation. This has to be taken into consideration. He stylises his works in the same manner as that in which (varying according to the personality of their genius) the douanier Rousseau, Picasso, Matisse, Derain, Modigliani, Stravinsky, Debussy, stylise, or have stylised, theirs. That is all; if we grasp that fact the whole matter becomes easy. What may appear difficult is the habit of forming abstract patterns in words. We have long been accustomed to abstract patterns in the pictorial art, and to the idea that music is an abstract art, but nobody to my knowledge has ever gone so far in making abstract patterns in words as the modernist poet has. The nearest approach known to me is Beddoes:

> "Adam, that old carrion-crow
> Of Cairo."

There is, of necessity, a connecting thread running through each pattern, otherwise it would not be a pattern. But I can understand that the person who does not realise the necessity of cultivating all the possibilities of words as a medium—of understanding that medium—may be puzzled.

Let us take the case of Miss Gertrude Stein, who, although she is a prose-writer and not a poet, is an admirable example of the case in point. Miss Stein is bringing back life to our language by what appears, at first, to be an anarchic process. First she breaks down the predestined groups of words, their sleepy family habits; then she rebrightens them, examines their texture, and builds them into new and vital shapes. When we read her first we are unaware of the rebuilding process; we notice only the general breaking down of that to which we are accustomed. Yet can anyone deny the beauty of this, from *The Portrait of Constance Fletcher*?

"Oh, the bells that are the same are not stirring and the languid grace is not out of place and the older fur is disappearing. There is not such an end. If it had happened that the little flower was larger and the white colour was deeper and the silent light was darker and the passage was rougher, it would have been as it was and the triumph was in the place where the light was bright

and the beauty was not losing having that posses-
sion. That was not what was tenderly. This was
the piece of the health that was strange when there
was the disappearance that had not any origin.
The darkness was not the same. There was the
writing and the preparation that was pleasing and
succeeding and being enterprising. It was not sub-
dued when there was discussion, it was done when
there was the room that was not a dream."

The question of the making of abstract patterns
is far more important at this time than any question of whether free verse is on as high a level as
other forms of verse. To many people, heedless
of the fact that free verse is often most intricately
rhymed, the term "free verse" means merely an
absence of rhyme, and this, excepting in the case
of blank verse, appears to them iconoclastic. Yet
even in the late sixteenth and early seventeenth
centuries there were quarrels between poets and
men of letters as to whether rhyme gives an addi-
tional beauty to verse; so the absence of rhyme is
not in itself iconoclastic, though, in the centuries
of which I speak, it appeared strange to some.
Milton, in his Preface to *Paradise Lost* (1668),
says:

"Rhyme (is) . . . no necessary adjunct or true ornament of poem or good verse, in longer works especially, but the invention of a barbarous age, to set off wretched matter and lame metre; graced indeed since by the use of some famous modern poets, carried away by custom, but much to their own vexation, hindrance, and constraint to express many things otherwise, and for the most part worse, than else they would have expressed them. Not without cause therefore, some, both Italian and Spanish poets of prime note, have rejected rhyme both in longer and shorter works, as have also long since our best English tragedies, as a thing of itself, to all judicious ears, trivial and of no true musical delight; which consists only in apt numbers, fit quantity of syllables, and the sense variously drawn out from one verse into another, not in the jingling sound of like endings, a fault avoided by the learned ancients both in poetry and all good oratory. This neglect then of rhyme so little is to be taken for a defect, though it may seem so perhaps to vulgar readers, that it rather is to be esteemed an example set, the first in English, of ancient liberty recovered to heroic poem from the troublesome and modern bondage of rhyming."

Yet the absence of rhyme is regarded by "vulgar readers" as a reason for deriding free verse. Would it be indiscreet to inquire if those self-appointed guardians of the purity of literature, the Yellow Press and the writers of lyrics for revues, believe blank verse to be in rhyme?

When we consider that it is a debatable point if a great part of *Samson Agonistes* is not in free verse, and that Blake wrote a defence of free verse, it appears to us as curious that this should be regarded as a modern invention. And why should it be supposed to be formless and without rhythm? The trouble is that the hearing of many people has become coarsened until they do not hear the rhythm excepting in the coarsest and most obvious forms. On this subject Coleridge, somewhere in his *Lectures,* says:

"The true ground of the mistake lies in confounding mechanical regularity with organic form. The form is mechanic, when on any given material we impress a predetermined form, not necessarily arising out of the properties of the material; as when to a mass of wet clay we give it whatever shape we wish it to retain when hardened. The organic form, on the other hand, is innate; it

33

shapes and it develops itself from within, and the fullness of its development is one and the same with the perfection of its outward form."

Poets of this time are beset by three parrot-cries from the press and the public. One—and this only comes from the most ignorant—is the cry of "free verse," used as a term of abuse and applied, often, to poets who work almost exclusively in couplets (a form much admired in the time of Samuel Johnson) and in quatrains. Another parrot-cry is "all technique and no great moral message." Yet one of the most urgent needs of our time is that there should be a fresh apprehension of the importance of technique. Poetry is primarily an art, and not a dumping-ground for emotions. When we are told that a poem cannot be a great poem unless it be built on a lofty moral theme, it is obvious that this belief is based on a total misapprehension of the nature of poetry. *The Rape of the Lock* is a great poem, though the theme is not lofty and contains no reference to morality. I have yet to discover the lofty moral message in any poem of Keats. Yet *Endymion* and *The Eve of St. Agnes* are great poems. Who can claim this for *Aurora Leigh*, though the theme is both lofty and moral! "Two kinds of dilettanti," says Goethe, "there are in poetry: he who neglects the indispensable mechanical part and thinks he has done enough if he shows spirituality and feeling; and he who seeks to arrive at poetry merely by mechanism, in which he can acquire an artist's readiness and is without soul and matter." And he adds that the first does most harm to art and the last to himself.

The third parrot-cry to which we are accustomed is that of "Poetry is meant to give pleasure." On this subject Wordsworth, in a letter to John Wilson (1800), says: "You begin . . . with this observation, that nothing is a fit subject for poetry which does not please. But here follows a question, Does not please whom? Some have little knowledge of natural imagery of any kind, and of course little relish for it; some are disgusted with the very mention of the words pastoral poetry, sheep or shepherds; some cannot tolerate a poem with a ghost or any supernatural agency in it; others would shrink from an animated description of the pleasures of love as from a thing carnal and libidinous; some cannot bear to see delicate and refined feelings ascribed to men in low conditions in society . . . others are disgusted with the naked language of some of the most interesting passions of men, because either it is indelicate, or gross, or vulgar. . . . Then there are professional and national prejudices for evermore. Some take no interest in the description of a particular passion or quality, as love of solitariness, we will say, genial activity of fancy, love of nature, religion, and so forth, because they have (little or) nothing of it in themselves; and so on without end. I return then to (the) question, Please whom? Or what?"

But why should we trouble to discuss these matters further? For what use can poetry be put to, and who cares what conclusions poets arrive at? As Peacock wrote in 1820, during the lifetime of Shelley and Keats:

"It (poetry) can never make a philosopher, nor a statesman, nor in any class of life a useful or rational man. It cannot claim the slightest share in any one of the comforts and utilities of life in which we have witnessed so many and such rapid advances. But, though not useful, it may be said it is highly ornamental and deserves to be cultivated for the pleasure it yields. Even if this be granted, it does not follow that a writer of poetry in the present state of society is not a waster of his own time and a robber of that of others. Poetry is not one of those arts which, like painting, require repetition and multiplication in order to be diffused among society. There are more good poems already existing than are sufficient to employ that portion of life which any mere reader and recipient of poetical impressions should devote to them, and these, having been produced in poetical times, are far superior in all the characteristics of poetry to the artificial reconstructions of a few morbid ascetics in unpoetical times. To read the promiscuous rubbish of the present time to the exclusion of the select treasures of the past is to substitute the worse for the better variety of the same mode of enjoyment.

"But in whatever degree poetry is cultivated, it must necessarily be to the neglect of some branch of useful study; and it is a lamentable spectacle to see minds, capable of better things, running to seed in the specious indolence of these empty, aimless mockeries of intellectual exertion. Poetry was the mental rattle that awakened the attention of intellect in the infancy of civil society; but for the maturity of mind to make a serious business of the playthings of its childhood is as absurd as for a full-grown man to rub his gums with coral and cry to be charmed to sleep by the jingle of silver bells."

37